KINGFISHER
READERS

level
1

Seals

Thea Feldman

KINGFISHER
NEW YORK

KINGFISHER
LONDON & NEW YORK

Copyright © Macmillan Publishers International Ltd 2015
Published in the United States by Kingfisher,
175 Fifth Ave., New York, NY 10010
Kingfisher is an imprint of Macmillan Children's Books, London.
All rights reserved.

Distributed in the U.S. and Canada by Macmillan,
175 Fifth Ave., New York, NY 10010

Library of Congress Cataloging-in-Publication data
has been applied for.

Series editor: Thea Feldman
Literacy consultant: Ellie Costa, Bank Street College, New York

978-0-7534-7223-1 (HB)
978-0-7534-7224-8 (PB)

Kingfisher books are available for special promotions
and premiums. For details contact: Special Markets
Department, Macmillan, 175 Fifth Ave.,
New York, NY 10010.

For more information, please visit
www.kingfisherbooks.com

Printed in China

9 8 7 6 5 4 3 2 1
1TR/0615/WKT/UNTD/105MA

Picture credits
The Publisher would like to thank the following for permission to reproduce their material.
Top = t; Bottom = b; Center = c; Left = l; Right = r
Cover Shutterstock/Bildagentur Zoonar GmbH; Pages 3 Naturepl/Bryan & Cherry Alexander;
4–5 FLPA/Minden Pictures/Norbert Wu; 6 Alamy/Wolfgang Polzer; 7 Alamy/Agencja Fotograficzna
Caro; 8 Shutterstock/Randimal; 9 FLPA/Samuel Blanc/Biosphoto; 10 Shutterstock/David Osborn;
11 Alamy/Andrey Nekrasov; 12 Getty/David Fleetham/Visuals Unlimited Inc., 13t Shutterstock/
CVancoillie; 13b FLPA/Imagebroker/Norbert Probst; 14 Alamy/Nature Picture Library; 15 Naturepl/
Doug Perrine; 16 Shutterstock/Volt Collection; 17 Shutterstock/duchy; 18–19 Alamy/Robert Harding
World Imagery; 20–21 Alamy/Steve Bloom Images; 22–23 Shutterstock/phodo; 24 Shutterstock/
bikeriderlondon; 25 Shutterstock/David Osborn; 26 Alamy/James Beards; 27 Alamy/imageBROKER;
28 Shutterstock/Steve Photography; 29 Alamy/imageBROKER; 30–31 Shutterstock/Stefan Simmerl.

Splash!

A seal dives into the water.

This seal can dive down
hundreds of feet.

It can hold its breath
for about 20 minutes!

How long can you hold
your breath?

A seal dives to look for food.

Seals eat fish, shrimp,
squid, and other animals.

There are many different
kinds of seal.

Some seals have spots.

Some seals have white bands.

The elephant seal is the
biggest seal.

The ringed seal is one
of the smallest seals.

Look at the body of this seal.

It is thick in the middle
and thinner at each end.

This shape helps the seal
move through water.

A seal has **flippers** instead of hands and feet!

Flippers help a seal move well in the water.

A seal can sleep in the water.

Some seals can even sleep under the water!

The holes in its **nostrils** close when a seal is under the water.

Most seals live in the **ocean**.

These seals live in a **lake**.

Many seals live where it is cold.

Some of them have thick fur to help keep them warm.

These seals are called fur seals.

Other seals have **blubber**
to help keep them warm.

Blubber is a thick layer
of fat under the skin.

Sometimes seals come out of the water and stay on land.

It is hard for seals
to move on land.

Fur seals push themselves forward with all four flippers.

This seal is sliding on its belly!

Why do seals come onto land?

They come to **mate** and have baby seals.

A male seal is called a **bull**.

A female seal is called a **cow**.

Sometimes bulls fight other bulls.

A baby seal is called a **pup**.
A cow has one pup at a time.

A mother leaves
her pup when it is
two weeks old.

The pup stays on land for
a few more weeks.

Then it is ready to swim.

Splash!

Glossary

blubber the fat under the skin of a seal

bull a male seal

cow a female seal

flippers the hands and feet of a seal

lake a large area of water surrounded by land

mate to find a partner to have babies with

nostrils the holes in a seal's nose for breathing

ocean a very large area of salty water

pup a baby seal